Poems of Awakening

"In this New Age, we tend to forget that the word 'spirit' refers to the vital force than animates us and creates our consciousness. Thus, at its best, 'spiritual' poetry is poetry that takes on questions of the most profound and elemental nature. *Poems of Awakening* is an ambitious collection that grapples with these questions from many different perspectives: personal, religious, historical. It's a rich and surprising book."

CHASE TWICHELL

Poems of Awakening

EDITED BY
BETSY SMALL

Outskirts Press, Inc.
Denver, Colorado

Cover Photo: RACHEL SMALL
Author Photo: SARAH SMALL
Book Design: CYNTHIA BERKSHIRE

Outskirts Press, Inc.
http://www.outskirtspress.com

ISBN: 978-1-4327-3434-3

Outskirts Press and the "OP" logo
are trademarks belonging to Outskirts Press, Inc.

PRINTED IN THE UNITED STATES OF AMERICA

ACKNOWLEDGMENTS

First and foremost I wish to dedicate *Poems of Awakening* to the
memory of my beloved niece, Naomi Shea (1968-2010), who kept
this book on her night table and inspired me over and over with her
passion for the poems. I would also like to express gratitude to my
yoga teacher trainer Maya Breuer, who deepened my love of yoga and
linked it to poetry, to Amy Weintraub for her infectious enthusiasm
during the early stages of the anthology, and to friends, colleagues and
poets whose appreciation of the book motivated me to keep focused in
spite of frustrations during the tedious work of gaining permissions.
I also wish to extend special thanks to Eileen Moeller and Chase Twichell
for their editorial advice and warm encouragement, my sister Judy Shea
for her keen eye and invaluable honesty, John Stifler for his concise
editing skills, and my book designer Cynthia Berkshire for her expertise,
patience and flexibility. I cannot stress enough the gratitude I feel
toward my immediate family for their loving support — Rachel's
generous and insightful editing assistance, Sarah's passionate belief
in my capabilities and Hal's devoted and balanced presence during the
long course of creating this book.

I am also grateful to the editors and authors of several outstanding
anthologies of spiritual poetry who inspired me by example. *(see back
section:* RECOMMENDED ANTHOLOGIES*)*

CONTENTS

❧

INTRODUCTION

Poems of Awakening is an international anthology in which poets speak about their experiences of living joyfully in the moment and sensing themselves as part of what Walt Whitman calls "a vast similitude" which "interlocks all." Although the poets belong to a diversity of religions such as Christianity, Judaism, Islam (Sufism), Hinduism and Buddhism, others are unaffiliated with any religion or belief system, and all have written poems that open windows through which to view that which is eternal. Although their awakened perceptions transcend that which can ordinarily be described in words, the poets come close to conveying this essence with the magic of their craft, naming their understandings in both universal and unique ways: God, Buddha, Love, "Creator Spirit," "the never to be spoken word," "one whole voice that is you," "the invisible lifebird," "the great starry void," "the grace of the world" and more.

In the summer of 2007 I had been practicing yoga every day for several months and found myself gradually opening up to emotions that had been buried as tension in my body, as well as experiencing glimmers of spirituality. One day as I searched on a beach for rocks to add to my collection, I felt a smile radiating through me, along with a question: "Why would I want to own these rocks if they are already a part of me, and I a part of them?" I had shifted into a state of deep bliss, sensing myself as one with the sea, sky, and earth, tiny in comparison to it all, bursting with happiness and at the same time profoundly calm. I remember thinking, "Now I know what people are experiencing when they speak of God." Soon this extraordinary state faded and I lined my pockets with rocks for my collection, but my life's direction had changed.

Soon after this I resolved to become a yoga teacher so I could share with others the joyful openings I had discovered through this timeless practice. During my teacher training the seeds for Poems of Awakening were sown. As we lay down in Savasana, a yoga practice of profound relaxation, our teacher, Maya Breuer, would recite the poetry of Danna Faulds:

> *Just for now, without*
> *Asking how, let yourself*
> *Sink into stillness. Just*
> *For now, lay down the*
> *Weight you so patiently*
> *Bear upon your shoulders.*
> *Feel the earth receive*
> *You, and the infinite*
> *Expanse of sky grow even*
> *Wider as your awareness*
> *Reaches up to meet it...*

These words recalled my awakening on the beach, and I became inspired to search for other similarly moving poems to gather into a collection to be read during savasana, which I presented as my final project for the training.

I was grateful to discover that the anthology appealed to many more kinds of people than yogis, and I dedicated the years that followed to creating a book of optimistic poetry that could inspire a broad range of people, from the deeply religious to those with no spiritual affiliation and from those with little patience for poetry to seasoned poetry-lovers. Since awakenings are felt rather than taught, I have steered away from poems that philosophize or preach in favor of ones that woo the reader into the heart and core of each writer's experience through image or example.

The anthology is organized as a journey through various kinds of awakening, from everyday experiences of deep awareness to the visionary insights of great mystics. Each of the seven sets opens with a few ancient poems and continues with contemporary poetry, and each set contains its own narrative arc that flows thematically into the next. The reader can savor poems individually, as integral elements of sets, or as part of the entire collection, which can be read in one sitting as a poetic essay consisting of linked sets.

I. MY BODY EFFERVESCES
In yoga tradition the first step to preparing the mind for meditation is to focus awareness on the body. This set celebrates the body as sanctuary.

II. A DEEP QUIET – STILLNESS AND LIGHT
Poems in this set describe co-existing states of stillness and luminescence attained through meditation, communion with nature, or slowing down the pace of one's life to experience the moment.

III. NOW I BECOME MYSELF
Here poets render their journeys toward finding the "true self," which they discover within themselves or by merging with the higher consciousness that unites all.

IV. HEALING & RENEWAL
In this set poets express optimism in the face of suffering and loss, taking comfort in the knowledge of nature's cycles.

V. MAY MY HEART ALWAYS BE OPEN
These poems reveal facets of love that nourish and sustain us: infatuation, erotic love, marital love, the bond between parent and child, and reverence for all things.

VI. HOW A BEAUTIFUL DAY IS SPENT
Here poets savor everyday living. Work is transformed into exploration, the mundane becomes sacred, and each day presents new opportunities for gratitude.

VII. THE ALL-SURROUNDING GRACE
This set contains poets' diverse renderings of their encounters with grace. Although these experiences can be fleeting, each opens up a lasting sense of connection to the universe.

I. My Body Effervesces

"There is a gem in the mountain of your body,
seek that mine."

JALĀL AD-DĪN RŪMĪ

HIDING IN THIS CAGE
Kabir *translated by Sushil Rao*

Hiding in this cage
of visible matter

is the invisible
lifebird

pay attention
to her

she is singing
your song

STILL THE BODY *(excerpt)*
Kabir *translated by Sushil Rao*

still the body
still the mind
still the voice inside

in silence
feel the stillness move

WHEN THE AUTUMN WIND
Izumi Shikibu *translated by Jane Hirshfield with Mariko Aratani*

When the autumn wind
blows down from Tokiwa Mountain,
my body fills, as if blushing,
with the color and scent
of pine.

I TALK TO MY BODY
Anna Swir translated by Czeslaw Milosz & Leonard Nathan

My body, you are an animal
whose appropriate behavior
Is concentration and discipline.
An effort
of an athlete, of a saint and of a yogi.

Well trained
you may become for me
a gate
through which I will leave myself
and a gate
through which I will enter myself.
A plumb line to the center of the earth
and a cosmic ship to Jupiter.

My body, you are an animal
for whom ambition
is right.
Splendid possibilities
are open to us.

SAINT ANIMAL
Chase Twichell

Suddenly it was clear to me —
I was something I hadn't been before.
It was as if the animal part of my being

had reached some kind of maturity that gave it
authority, and had begun to use it.

I thought about death for two years.
My animal flailed and tore at its cage
till I let it go. I watched it

drift out into the easy eddies of twilight
and then veer off, not knowing me.

I'm not a bird but I'm inhabited by a spirit
that's uplifting me. It's my animal, my saint
and soldier, my flame of yearning,

come back to tell me
what it was like to be without me.

GREAT AS YOU ARE
Susan Griffin

Be like a bear in the forest of yourself.
Even sleeping you are powerful in your breath.
Every hair has life
and standing, as you do, swaying
from one foot to the other
all the forest stands with you.
Each minute sound, one after another,
is distinct in your ear. Here
in the blur of mixed sensations, you can
feel the crisp outline of being, particulate.
Great as you are, huge as you are and
growling like the deepest drum,
the continual vibration that makes music
what it is,
not some light stone skipped on the surface of things,
you travel below
sounding the depths where only the dauntless go.
Be like the bear and
do not forget
how you rounded your
massive shape over the just ripened
berry which burst
in your mouth that moment
how you rolled in
the wet grass, cool and silvery, mingling
with your sensate skin,
how you shut
your eyes and swam far and farther
still, starlight
shaping itself to your body,
starship rocking the grand, slow waves
under the white trees, in the
snowy night.

PRAYER *(excerpts)*
Lisa Colt

May we reveal our abundance without shame.
May we peel back our sleeping wintery layers
like snakeskins, like the silk chrysalis,
like clothing cast off during love.
May we unravel with abandon like lover's knots
before knitting ourselves back to the heart.
May we settle into our own rhythms as tides do —
within the borders of the moon's calling...
May the milky fingers of the moon
reach down nightly to cherish and unveil us.
May we turn our bodies generously in its light
like tranquil fish glinting underwater,
like precious stones...

YOU THERE...
Judith Barrington

Put the palms of your hands together
close to your body, thumbs touching your chest
then bow your head to the tree
whose body bears these words.

In the deep pool under the cedar
a trout rises to a mayfly and ripples spread
in widening O's like the years
etched into heartwood as it grows.

What have the years written into your body?
What pattern emerged as you passed through fire?
Put your palms together, lifeline to lifeline.
Bow your head for the history you bear.

THE STAMMER
Jean Nordhaus

We are two-minded, my tongue and I.
It is always like this: I mean
to say _That house is tall._
or God is one. But the tongue
has another opinion. It wants

to be heard. We are like Mishnah,
two sparrows disputing
a morsel of law. I grapple
with my tongue as Jacob
wrestled with the angel

for a word. From this clash
of intentions I've learned
to hold back, to listen:
the voice at my shoulder when I
try to speak, saying

Wait. The tongue
is a caged beast, an animal
wild to escape. Compel it,
and it will elude you. Released,
it will yield to your lightest

desire. Soft,
and the sounds that need
to speak themselves will flow.
Be gentle and the words will come like deer
to water or a woman to love.

WILD GEESE
Mary Oliver

You do not have to be good.
You do not have to walk on your knees
for a hundred miles through the desert, repenting.
You only have to let the soft animal of your body
    love what it loves.
Tell me about despair, yours, and I will tell you mine.
Meanwhile the world goes on.
Meanwhile the sun and the clear pebbles of the rain
are moving across the landscapes,
over the prairies and the deep trees,
the mountains and the rivers.
Meanwhile the wild geese, high in the clean blue air,
are heading home again.
Whoever you are, no matter how lonely,
the world offers itself to your imagination,
calls to you like the wild geese, harsh and exciting —
over and over announcing your place
in the family of things.

NAKED WITH THE LEOPARDS
Ellie Schoenfeld

When I close my eyes
it is not February.
I am not in Duluth
and these women in concert
with their drums
along with the rest of us
are in Kenya.
It is warm
and we are dancing
In the sunlight
until Zuni is talking something
about night runners
who run naked with the leopards
so now it is night
and I have added a large fire,
subtracted our clothes.
Leopard eyes flash at the edges.
There is a distracting moment
when I think, "Even if it was warm here
there would be mosquitoes and what kinds
of insects live in Kenya?
I concentrate on returning
to the circle, notice
that I have given myself
a different body,
thin and muscular.
I roll my eyes and add a few pounds,
remove that muscle tone, those cheekbones.
The varicose veins and cellulite
take a whole extra song
but finally they too
join the dance
and when the applause arrives
I have stopped flinching.
The real me sweats and laughs
then runs into the forest,
vanishes with the leopards.

ON SWIMMING
Adam Zagajewski

The rivers of this country are sweet
as a troubadour's song,
the heavy sun wanders westward
on yellow circus wagons.
Little village churches
hold a fabric of silence so fine
and old that even a breath
could tear it.
I love to swim in the sea, which keeps
talking to itself
in the monotone of a vagabond
who no longer recalls
exactly how long he's been on the road.
Swimming is like prayer:
palms join and part,
join and part,
almost without end.

SAVASANA
Peggy Hong

swimming into stillness forget
tomorrow forsake
yesterday

air enters and leaves
careless breath ushers
space of nothing

body spreads
a perfect circle
into forgiving earth
mountains grow deeper underground

blood and lymph pulse in saline
purge sedimental attachments

settle into nameless
breezed clean mind

SABBATH POEM (1990 – V)
Wendell Berry

The body in the invisible
Familiar room accepts the gift
Of sleep, and for a while is still;
Instead of will, it lives by drift

In the great night that gathers up
The earth and sky. Slackened, unbent,
Unwanting, without fear or hope,
The body rests beyond intent.

Sleep is the prayer the body prays,
Breathing in unthought faith the Breath
That through our worry-wearied days
Preserves our rest, and is our truth.

FALLING ASLEEP
Anna Swir translated by *Czeslaw Milosz & Leonard Nathan*

I yawn,
I stretch,
I stretch out,
I stretch all over
in my body
as in a large, luxurious sleeping bag.

And then I fall
down,
down
to the bottom of happiness.

THIS BODY
Michael Cuddihy

Each time breath draws through me,
I know it's older than we are.
The haggard pine that watches by the door
Was here even before my older brothers.
It's a feeling I get when I pick up a stone
And look at it's mottled skin, the grey
Sleeve of time.
        This body I use,
Rooted here, this hillside, leaves shaking in wind,
Was once as small as a stone
And lived inside a woman.
These words, even–––
They've come such a long way to find me.
But the sleep that translates everything
Moves in place, unwearied, the whole weight of Ocean
That left us here breathless.

MY BODY EFFERVESCES
Anna Swir   *translated by Czeslaw Milosz & Leonard Nathan*

I am born for the second time.
I am light
as the eyelash of the wind.
I am froth, I am froth.

I walk dancing,
if I wish, I will soar.
The condensed lightness
of my body
condenses most forcibly
in the lightness of my foot
and its five toes.
The foot skims the earth
which gives way like compressed air.
An elastic duo
of the earth and of the foot. A dance
of liberation.

I am born for the second time,
happiness of the world
came to me again.
My body effervesces.
I think with my body which effervesces.

If I wish
I will soar.

TERESA OF AVILA (1515-82)
Shara McCallum

When St. Teresa sings
the word blossoms
on her lips, the spine
of the world splinters
into song. When she moves
her hips, she is no saint
but a woman beneath
her cassock, orange as the stain
of the sun. She is not burlap
sacks chafing skin but silken
threads sewn whole.
St. Teresa is the breath
she speaks but
cannot understand:
notes that are sounds,
words divorced
from meaning, only the feeling
of the Latin vowel and consonant
opening and closing
against her throat, a bird fluttering
its wings inside her chest.
St. Teresa is her own redemption,
her body feeding the flock,
her tongue a wafer of its own.
The host, a consecration
of her light, her spirit
and flesh radiating
against the halls of the church,
illuminating its darkest holds.

GIRLS TAKE THEIR STANCES
Janet E. Aalfs

Girls take their stances
unwavering, bold
as the amaryllis flaring: *I am here.*
Each girl balances her own way,
soaked in the rain and sun
of a promise to live
full from the root.

Faces blossom
infinite grace. Together
they are a mountain
meadow, bells of light ringing in the wind: *Here, here*
their bodies chime, *We are here.*

EARTH
Derek Walcott

Let the day grow on you upward
through your feet,
the vegetal knuckles,

to your knees of stone,
until by evening you are a black tree;
feel, with evening,

the swifts thicken your hair,
the new moon rising out of your forehead,
and the moonlit veins of silver

running from your armpits
like rivulets under white leaves.
Sleep, as ants

cross over your eyelids.
You have never possessed anything
as deeply as this.

This is all you have owned
from the first outcry
through forever;

you can never be dispossessed.

EARTH YOUR DANCING PLACE
May Swenson

Beneath heaven's vault
remember always walking
through halls of cloud
down aisles of sunlight
or through high hedges
of the green rain
walk in the world
highheeled with swirl of cape
hand at the swordhilt
of your pride
Keep a tall throat
Remain aghast at life

Enter each day
as upon a stage
lighted and waiting
for your step
Crave upward as flame
have keenness in the nostril
Give your eyes
to agony or rapture

Train your hands
as birds to be
brooding or nimble
Move your body
as the horses
sweeping on slender hooves
over crag and prairie
with fleeing manes
and aloofness of their limbs

Take earth for your own large room
and the floor of earth
carpeted with sunlight
and hung round with silver wind
for your dancing place

II. A Deep Quiet – Stillness and Light

"In the attitude of silence the soul finds the path
in a clearer light."

MAHATMA GANDHI

NOT GOING, NOT COMING
Shih-Te *translated by Jerome Seaton*

not going, not coming
rooted, deep and still
not reaching out, not reaching in
just resting, at the center
a single jewel, the flawless crystal drop
in the blaze of its brilliance
the way beyond

SILENCE
Hafiz *translated by Daniel Ladinsky*

A day of Silence
Can be a pilgrimage in itself.

A day of Silence
Can help you listen
To the Soul play
Its marvelous lute and drum.

Is not most talking
A crazed defense of a crumbling fort?

I thought we came here
To surrender in Silence,

To yield to Light and Happiness,

To Dance within
In celebration of Love's Victory!

JUST DONE
Yuan Mei *translated by Jerome Seaton*

A month alone behind closed doors
forgotten books, remembered, clear again.
Poems come, like water to the pool
Welling,
                    up and out,
from perfect silence.

IT WAS BEGINNING WINTER *(part 5 from "The Lost Son")*
Theodore Roethke

It was beginning winter,
An in-between time,
The landscape still partly brown:
The bones of weeds kept swinging in the wind,
Above the blue snow.

It was beginning winter,
The light moved slowly over the frozen field,
Over the dry seed-crowns,
The beautiful surviving bones
Swinging in the wind.

Light traveled over the wide field;
Stayed.
The weeds stopped swinging.
The mind moved, not alone,
Through the clear air, in the silence.

    Was it light?
    Was it light within?
    Was it light within light?
    Stillness becoming alive,
    Yet still?

A lively understandable spirit
Once entertained you.
It will come again.
Be still.
Wait.

WHY THE SUN COMES UP
William Stafford

To be ready again if they find an owl, crows
choose any old tree before dawn and hold a convention
where they practice their outrage routine. "Let's elect
someone." "No, no! Forget it." They
see how many crows can dance on a limb.
"Hey, listen to this one." One old crow
flaps away off and looks toward the east. In that
lonely blackness God begins to speak
in a silence beyond all that moves. Delighted
wings move close and almost touch each other.
Everything stops for a minute, and the sun rises.

THE BUDDHA'S LAST INSTRUCTION
Mary Oliver

"Make of yourself a light,"
said the Buddha,
before he died.
I think of this every morning
as the east begins
to tear off its many clouds
of darkness, to send up the first
signal — a white fan
streaked with pink and violet,
even green.
An old man, he lay down
between two sala trees,
and he might have said anything,
knowing it was his final hour.
The light burns upward,
it thickens and settles over the fields.
Around him, the villagers gathered
and stretched forward to listen.
Even before the sun itself
hangs, disattached, in the blue air,
I am touched everywhere
by its ocean of yellow waves.
No doubt he thought of everything
that had happened in his difficult life.
And then I feel the sun itself
as it blazes over the hills,
like a million flowers on fire —
clearly I'm not needed,
yet I feel myself turning
into something of inexplicable value.
Slowly, beneath the branches,
he raised his head.
He looked into the faces of that frightened crowd.

THERE IS A LIGHT IN ME
Anna Swir translated by Czeslaw Milosz & Leonard Nathan

Whether in daytime or in nighttime
I always carry inside
a light.
In the middle of noise and turmoil
I carry silence.
Always
I carry light and silence.

SABBATH POEM (2001 – IV)
Wendell Berry

Ask the world to reveal its quietude—
not the silence of machines when they are still,
but the true quiet by which birdsongs,
trees, bellworts, snails, clouds, storms
become what they are, and are nothing else.

HUSH – –
Rolf Jacobsen translated by Roger Greenwald

Hush says the ocean.
Hush says the little wave at the shore — hush
not so violent, not
so proud not
so eager for attention.
Hush
say the breakers that
pile up at the headlands,
the surf at the beaches. Hush
they say to us —
it's our world
our eternity.

LOST
David Wagoner

Stand still. The trees ahead and bushes beside you
Are not lost. Wherever you are is called Here,
And you must treat it as a powerful stranger,
Must ask permission to know it and be known.
The forest breathes. Listen. It answers,
I have made this place around you.
If you leave it, you may come back again, saying Here.
No two trees are the same to Raven.
No two branches are the same to Wren.
If what a tree or a bush does is lost on you,
You are surely lost. Stand still. The forest knows
Where you are. You must let it find you.

OUT OF HIDING
Li-Young Lee

Someone said my name in the garden,

while I grew smaller
in the spreading shadow of the peonies,

grew larger by my absence to another,
grew older among the ants, ancient

under the opening heads of the flowers,
new to myself, and stranger.

When I heard my name again, it sounded far,
like the name of the child next door,
or a favorite cousin visiting for the summer,

while the quiet seemed my true name,
a near and inaudible singing
born of hidden ground.

Quiet to quiet, I called back.
And the birds declared my whereabouts all morning.

AFTER
G.F. Dutton

Not the sight of it
after the storm.
Not the oaks thrown, their
tangle of branches, not
the sun through them
steaming the long roof-tree,
still firm.
But the breath held,
the great light of it,
and a silence the sound
of a horseman's hand
soothing repeatedly
some tremble of haunches.

RIGHT BEHIND YOUR FOOT
Rolf Jacobsen   *translated by Olav Grinde*

Right behind your foot
is the greatest silence
and a wondrous love,
different from anything you know.

Different from all
that you can hear, you can see
— the song after your feet,
the light after your hands.

Right behind your shoulder,
closer than you think, a peace
you have not yet felt
where the world falls silent
one deep and sudden moment
as after an unspoken promise
through a closed mouth.

INVOCATION
Ursula K. Le Guin

O silence, my love silence,
I have feared you: my tongue
has rattled on my teeth
dreading to be dumb so long
when I am done with breath.
  And I have needed prattle,
kind blather, and the come and go
of voices, human voices,
the sky whose moon you are,
the ground whose flower.
  But I beseech you come,
now, my love silence, O
reward and freedom, balance
beyond choices, in whom alone is heard
the meditation of the twilight bird
and the never to be spoken word.

NEW YEAR RESOLVE
May Sarton

The time has come
To stop allowing the clutter
To clutter my mind
Like dirty snow,
Shove it off and find
Clear time, clear water.
Time for a change,
Let silence in like a cat
Who has sat at my door
Neither wild nor strange
Hoping for food from my store
And shivering on the mat.
Let silence in.
She will rarely mew,
She will sleep on my bed
And all I have ever been
Either false or true
Will live again in my head.
For it is now or not
As old age silts the stream,
To shove away the clutter,
To untie every knot,
To take the time to dream,
To come back to still water.

III. Now I Become Myself

"Go where you can find your beloved,
where you can find yourself."

THICH NHAT HANH

YOU WHO WANT KNOWLEDGE
Hadewijch II *translated by Jane Hirshfield*

You who want
knowledge,
seek the Oneness
within
There you
will find
the clear mirror
already waiting

WATCHING THE MOON
Izumi Shikibu *translated by Jane Hirshfield & Mariko Aratani*

Watching the moon
at midnight,
solitary, mid-sky,
I knew myself completely,
no part left out.

AMIDST THE NOTES OF MY KOTO
Akiko Yosano *translated by Kenneth Rexroth*

Amidst the notes
Of my koto is another
Deep mysterious tone,
A sound that comes from
Within my own breast.

SONG OF THE OPEN ROAD *(excerpt from part 5)*
Walt Whitman

From this hour I ordain myself loos'd of limits and imaginary lines,
Going where I list, my own master, total and absolute,
Listening to others, considering well what they say,
Pausing, searching, receiving, contemplating,
Gently, but with undeniable will, divesting myself of the holds that
    would hold me.

I inhale great draughts of space;
The east and the west are mine, and the north and the south are mine.

I am larger, better than I thought,
I did not know I held so much goodness...

PRICELESS GIFTS

Anna Swir translated by Czeslaw Milosz & Leonard Nathan

An empty day without events.
And that is why
it grew immense
as space. And suddenly
happiness of being
entered me.

I heard
in my heartbeat
the birth of time
and each instant of life
one after the other
came rushing in
like priceless gifts.

TRURO
Elizabeth Spires

I found a white stone on the beach
inlaid with a blue-green road I could not follow.
All night I'd slept in fits and starts,
my only memory the in-out, in-out, of the tide.
And then morning. And then a walk,
the white stone beckoning, glinting in the sun.
I felt its calm power as I held it
and wished a wish I cannot tell.
It fit in my hand like a hand gently
holding my hand through a sleepless night.
A stone, so like, so unlike,
all the others it could only be mine.

The wordless white stone of my life!

THE WOMAN IN THE ORDINARY
Marge Piercy

The woman in the ordinary pudgy downcast girl
is crouching with eyes and muscles clenched.
Round and pebble smooth she effaces herself
under ripples of conversation and debate.
The woman in the block of ivory soap
has massive thighs that neigh,
great breasts that blare and strong arms that trumpet.
The woman of the golden fleece
laughs uproariously from the belly
inside the girl who imitates
a Christmas card virgin with glued hands,
who fishes for herself in other's eyes,
who stoops and creeps to make herself smaller.
In her bottled up is a woman peppery as curry,
a yam of a woman of butter and brass,
compounded of acid and sweet like a pineapple,
like a handgrenade set to explode,
like goldenrod ready to bloom.

NOISY FALLING IN
Janet E. Aalfs

Not long ago in another life the girl
fell in. Conviction and all
that sunshine melting her stiff

upper lip. Generations
in a string of tiny beads
she threaded breathing on a needle,

thin as a hair. And the constant
running across the square
of patchy grass, eyes closed.

So much cause, she forgot
to stop. The water of Buttonwood
Pond, though full of weeds and aluminum

fliptops, felt soft to her plunging
feet. She could have avoided
the spectacle, undone

her dreaming. Apple blossoms floated
like spring snowflakes, her hair shining.
Could have held on

in the usual fashion, reining
back, caught at the throat
of whiplash one more time. But the wound up

works let loose propelling through shallows…
She refused to give up
wings. Gold wind turned her eyelids

crimson and swirls of black
like the universe lived
inside. Her body opening fell

then rose in sputters awake, noisy
as the flock of mallards
she startled into flight.

ON PUTNAM BROOK BRIDGE
Pamela Cranston

Built with strapping boards,
two planks wide,
plain as a backwoods church,
it straddled Putnam Brook
like a swaggering lumberjack,
betting Nature to beat it down.

Underneath, pale Indian pipes
lifted their ghostly heads
from their moist burial mounds.
Beetles skittered across
the smooth skin of black water
like self-willed hockey pucks.

At twilight, a coterie of deer
tripped timidly down the trail,
hock-high in hobblebush flowers.
Sniffing danger, they turned to stone,
stared, then stayed
to nose the spilling stream.

Alone, caroled by summer crickets,
I would lean on the rail,
gazing into the dark, star-dusted sky,
and wonder how my life,
like a cinnamon fern,
would uncurl itself.

Forty years gone, would I care
about the crazy course
of water bugs on the river
or know how to be still
as the patient
wild doe?

Would I remember to hear
the silver music of birches,
whispering like girls in the midday wind?

In spite of danger,
would I dare to drink deeply
from my own stream?

WAITING
Leza Lowitz

You keep waiting for something to happen,
the thing that lifts you out of yourself,

catapults you into doing all the things you've put off
the great things you're meant to do in your life,

but somehow never quite get to.
You keep waiting for the planets to shift

the new moon to bring news,
the universe to align, something to give.

Meanwhile, the piles of papers, the laundry, the dishes, the job —
it all stacks up while you keep hoping

for some miracle to blast down upon you,
scattering the piles to the winds.

Sometimes you lie in bed, terrified of your life.
Sometimes you laugh at the privilege of waking.

But all the while, life goes on in its messy way.
And then you turn forty. Or fifty. Or sixty…

and some part of you realizes you are not alone
and you find signs of this in the animal kingdom —

when a snake sheds its skin its eyes glaze over,
it slinks under a rock, not wanting to be touched,

and when caterpillar turns to butterfly
if the pupa is brushed, it will die —

and when the bird taps its beak hungrily against the egg
it's because the thing is too small, too small,

and it needs to break out.
And midlife walks you into that wisdom

that this is what transformation looks like —
the mess of it, the tapping at the walls of your life,

the yearning and writhing and pushing,
until one day, one day

you emerge from the wreck
embracing both the immense dawn

and the dusk of the body,
glistening, beautiful

just as you are.

THE JOURNEY
Mary Oliver

One day you finally knew
what you had to do, and began,
though the voices around you
kept shouting
their bad advice—
though the whole house
began to tremble
and you felt the old tug
at your ankles.
"Mend my life!"
each voice cried.
But you didn't stop.
You knew what you had to do,
though the wind pried
with its stiff fingers
at the very foundations —
though their melancholy
was terrible.
It was already late
enough, and a wild night,
and the road full of fallen
branches and stones.
But little by little,
as you left their voices behind,
the stars began to burn
through the sheets of clouds,
and there was a new voice,
which you slowly
recognized as your own,
that kept you company
as you strode deeper and deeper
into the world,
determined to do
the only thing you could do—
determined to save
the only life you could save.

I FOUND IT

Fadwa Tuqan *translated by P. A. Byrne, S. Jayyusi & Naomi S. Nye*

I found it on a radiant day
after a long drifting.
It was green and blossoming
as the sun over palm trees
scattered golden bouquets;
April was generous that season
with loving and sun.

I found it
after a long wandering.
It was a tender evergreen bough
where birds took shelter,
a bough bending gently under storms
which later was straight again,
rich with sap,
never snapping in the wind's hand.
It stayed supple
as if there were no bad weather,
echoing the brightness of stars,
the gentle breeze,
the dew and the clouds.

I found it
on a vivid summer day
after a long straying,
a tedious search.
It was a quiet lake
where thirsty human wolves
and swirling winds could only briefly
disturb the waters.
Then they would clear again like crystal
to be the moon's mirror,
swimming place of light and blue,
bathing pool for the guardian stars.

I found it!
And now when the storms wail
and the face of the sun is masked in clouds,
when my shining fate revolves to dark,
my light will never be extinguished!
Everything that shadowed my life
wrapping it with night after night
has disappeared, lain down
in memory's grave,
since the day
my soul found
my soul.

TURNING
Lucille Clifton

turning into my own
turning on in
to my own self
at last
turning out of the
white cage, turning out of the
lady cage
turning at last
on a stem like a black fruit
in my own season
at last

UNHOLY SONNET
Mark Jarman

Blessedness — not only in a face
But in the air surrounding everybody,
The charged air that makes me see a body
As blessed just because it has a face.
To feel like that, thoroughly and wholly,
Because someone has just become herself,
Because in seeing I've become myself,
A halved reality completed, wholly.
And then to look at everyone this way,
Like a messenger sending forth a ray
Of gilded light that everywhere announces
That everything is pregnant with itself.
"Rejoice!" I want to say. "You are yourself."
And the mask of meanness turns aside and winces.

LOVE AFTER LOVE
Derek Walcott

The time will come
when, with elation,
you will greet yourself arriving
at your own door, in your own mirror,
and each will smile at the other's welcome,

and say, sit here. Eat.
You will love again the stranger who was your self.
Give wine. Give bread. Give back your heart
to itself, to the stranger who has loved you

all your life, whom you ignored
for another, who knows you by heart.
Take down the love letters from the bookshelf,

the photographs, the desperate notes,
peel your own image from the mirror.
Sit. Feast on your life.

NOW I BECOME MYSELF
May Sarton

Now I become myself. It's taken
Time, many years and places;
I have been dissolved and shaken,
Worn other people's faces,
Run madly, as if Time were there,
Terribly old, crying a warning,
"Hurry, you will be dead before--"
(What? Before you reach the morning?
Or the end of the poem is clear?
Or love safe in the walled city?)
Now to stand still, to be here,
Feel my own weight and density!
The black shadow on the paper
Is my hand; the shadow of a word
As thought shapes the shaper
Falls heavy on the page, is heard.
All fuses now, falls into place
From wish to action, word to silence,
My work, my love, my time, my face
Gathered into one intense
Gesture of growing like a plant.
As slowly as the ripening fruit
Fertile, detached, and always spent,
Falls but does not exhaust the root,
So all the poem is, can give,
Grows in me to become the song,
Made so and rooted by love.
Now there is time and Time is young.
O, in this single hour I live
All of myself and do not move.
I, the pursued, who madly ran,
Stand still, stand still, and stop the sun!

IV. Healing & Renewal

"Hope is the struggle of the soul, breaking loose from what is perishable, and attesting her eternity."

HERMAN MELVILLE

A NIGHT ON THE RIVER
Meng Hao-jan *translated by Sam Hamil*

Moored in island mist,
as the sun sets, a traveler's grief arises.

Beyond the great plain, the sky closes on trees.
On this gentle river, the moon arrives.

ON THE SPIRIT OF THE HEART AS MOON-DISK
Kojiju *translated by Edwin A. Cranston*

    Merely to know
The Flawless Moon dwells pure
    In the human heart
Is to find the Darkness of the night
Vanished under clearing skies.

WHEN THERE'S NO SIGN OF HOPE
Jalal ad-Din Rumi *translated by Zara Houshmand*

When there's no sign of hope in the desert,
So much hope still lives inside despair.
Heart, don't kill that hope: Even willows bear
Sweet fruit in the garden of the soul.

LIKE BARLEY BENDING
Sara Teasdale

Like barley bending
  In low fields by the sea,
Singing in hard wind
  Ceaselessly;

Like barley bending
  And rising again,
So would I, unbroken,
  Rise from pain;

So would I softly,
  Day long, night long,
Change my sorrow
  Into song.

FIRE FLOWERS
Emily Pauline Johnson (Tekahionwake)

And only where the forest fires have sped,
    Scorching relentlessly the cool north lands,
A sweet wild flower lifts its purple head,
And, like some gentle spirit sorrow-fed,
    It hides the scars with almost human hands.

And only to the heart that knows of grief,
    Of desolating fire, of human pain,
There comes some purifying sweet belief,
Some fellow-feeling beautiful, if brief.
    And life revives, and blossoms once again.

SONNET 2 FROM "THE AUTUMN SONNETS"
May Sarton

If I can let you go as trees let go
Their leaves, so casually, one by one;
If I can come to know what they do know,
That fall is the release, the consummation,
Then fear of time and the uncertain fruit
Would not distemper the great lucid skies
This strangest autumn, mellow and acute.
If I can take the dark with open eyes
And call it seasonal, not harsh or strange
(For love itself may need a time of sleep),
And, treelike, stand unmoved before the change,
Lose what I lose to keep what I can keep,
The strong root still alive under the snow,
Love will endure — if I can let you go.

MAY for Marian
Kerry Hardie

The blessèd stretch and ease of it —
heart's ease. The hills blue. All the flowering weeds
bursting open. Balm in the air. The birdsong
bouncing back out of the sky. The cattle
lain down in the meadow, forgetting to feed.
The horses swishing their tails.
The yellow flare of furze on the near hill.
And the first cream splatters of blossom
high on the thorns where the day rests longest.

All hardship, hunger, treachery of winter
forgotten.
This unfounded conviction: forgiveness, hope.

DEPRESSED BY A BOOK OF BAD POETRY, I WALK TOWARDS AN UNUSED PASTURE AND INVITE THE INSECTS TO JOIN ME
James Wright

Relieved, I let the book fall behind a stone.
I climb a slight rise of grass.
I do not want to disturb the ants
Who are walking single file up the fence post,
Carrying small white petals,
Casting shadows so frail that I can see through them.
I close my eyes for a moment, and listen.
The old grasshoppers
Are tired, they leap heavily now,
Their thighs are burdened.
I want to hear them, they have clear sounds to make.
Then lovely, far off, a dark cricket begins
In the maple trees.

THE DOOR
Jane Hirshfield

A note waterfalls steadily
through us,
just below hearing.

Or this early light
streaming through dusty glass:
what enters, enters like that,
unstoppable gift.

And there is also the other,
the breath-space held between any call
and its answer —

In the querying
first scuff of footstep,
the wood owls' repeating,
the two-counting heart:

A little sabbath,
minnow whose brightness silvers past time.

The rest-note,
unwritten,
hinged between worlds,
that precedes change and allows it.

A JOURNEY
Edward Field

When he got up that morning everything was different:
He enjoyed the bright spring day
But he did not realize it exactly, he just enjoyed it.

And walking down the street to the railroad station
Past magnolia trees with dying flowers like old socks
It was a long time since he had breathed so simply.

Tears filled his eyes and it felt good
But he held them back
Because men didn't walk around crying in that town.

Waiting on the platform at the station
The fear came over him of something terrible about to happen:
The train was late and he recited the alphabet to keep hold.

And in its time it came screeching in
And as it went on making its usual stops,
People coming and going, telephone poles passing,

He hid his head behind a newspaper
No longer able to hold back the sobs, and willed his eyes
To follow the rational weavings of the seat fabric.

He didn't do anything violent as he had imagined.
He cried for a long time, but when he finally quieted down
A place in him that had been closed like a fist was open,

And at the end of the ride he stood up and got off that train:
And through the streets and in all the places he lived in later on
He walked, himself at last, a man among men,
With such radiance that everyone looked up and wondered.

NOT WITHOUT LONGING
Karen Benke

Come, rest
inside this house
you left
to travel
so far. Home
now, you see
the sleeping mountain
was here all along —
the braided rope of the past
no longer someone else
you must look for. The heart
left open will heal itself,
a new moon rising.

THE UNBROKEN
Rashani Réa

There is a brokenness
out of which comes the unbroken,
a shatteredness
out of which blooms the unshatterable.

There is a sorrow
beyond all grief which leads to joy
and a fragility
out of whose depths emerges strength.

There is a hollow space
too vast for words
through which we pass with each loss,
out of whose darkness
we are sanctioned into being.

There is a cry deeper than all sound
whose serrated edges cut the heart
as we break open to the place inside
which is unbreakable and whole,
while learning to sing.

FOR WARMTH
Thich Nhat Hanh

I hold my face in my two hands.
No, I am not crying.
I hold my face in my two hands
to keep the loneliness warm —
two hands protecting,
two hands nourishing,
two hands preventing
my soul for leaving me
in anger.

BLESS THE TORN
Eileen D. Moeller

Bless the torn
part of each day,
the ruptures in us
that caused it
to tear where it did.

Bless the green
heart of each rupture,
the small green
kernel of hope
saved for replanting.

IN LOVE WITH THE NEW SUN
Ivan M. Granger

in love with the new sun
the cherry blossom forgets
the night's frost

THE FOUNTAIN
Denise Levertov

Don't say, don't say there is no water
to solace the dryness at our hearts.
I have seen

the fountain springing out of the rock wall
and you drinking there. And I too
before your eyes

found footholds and climbed
to drink the cool water.

The woman of that place, shading her eyes,
frowned as she watched — but not because
she grudged the water,

only because she was waiting
to see we drank our fill and were
refreshed.

Don't say, don't say there is no water.
That fountain is there among its scalloped
green and gray stones,

it is still there and always there
with its quiet song and strange power
to spring in us,

up and out through the rock.

THE EARLY BIRD
Ted Kooser

Still dark, and raining hard
on a cold May morning

and yet the early bird
is out there chirping,

chirping its sweet-sour
wooden-pulley notes,

pleased, it would seem,
to be given work,

hauling the heavy
bucket of dawn

up from the darkness,
note over note,

and letting us drink.

WALKERS WITH THE DAWN
Langston Hughes

Being walkers with the dawn and morning,
Walkers with the sun and morning,
We are not afraid of night,
Nor days of gloom,
Nor darkness —
Being walkers with the sun and morning.

V. May My Heart Always Be Open

"Openness — the heart's pure, unconditional yes
— is love's essence."

JOHN WELWOOD

LIFT THE VEIL
Kabir *translated by Sushil Rao*

lift the veil
that obscures
the heart

and there
you will find
what you are
looking for

FIRE
Muhyiddin Ibn 'Arabi *translated by Reynold A. Nicolson*

O Marvel! a garden amidst flames!
My heart has become capable of every form:
it is a pasture for gazelles and a convent for Christian monks,
and a temple for idols, and the pilgrim's Ka'ba,
and the tables of the Torah and the book of the Qur'an.
I follow the religion of Love: whatever way
Love's camels take, that is my religion and my faith.

NO RELIGION
Jalāl ad-Dīn Rūmī *translated by Shahram Shiva*

Last night,
I saw the realm of joy and pleasure.
There I melted like salt;
no religion, no blasphemy,
no conviction or uncertainty remained.
In the middle of my heart,
a star appeared,
and the seven heavens were lost in its
brilliance.

IT SPEAKS TO ME IN THE SILENCE OF THIS ONE
Fakhruddin Iraqi translated by *William C. Chittick & Peter Lamborn Wilson*

It speaks to me in the silence of this one
then through the words of that one speaking;

it whispers to me through an eyebrow raised
and the message of an eye winking.

And do you know what words it breathes into my ear? It says,

"I am Love: in heaven and earth I have no place;
I am the Wondrous Phoenix whose spoor cannot be traced.

With eyebrow-bow and arrow-winks I hunt
both worlds — and yet my weapons cannot be found.

Like the sun I brighten each atom's cheek;
I cannot be pinpointed: I am too manifest.

I speak with every tongue, listen with all ears,
but marvel at this: My ears and tongue are erased.

Since in all the world only I exist
above and below, no likeness of me can be found."

HE WHO KNOWS LOVE
Elsa Barker

He who knows Love   becomes Love, and his eyes
Behold Love in the heart of everyone,
  Even the loveless: as the light of the sun
Is one with all it touches. He is wise
With undivided wisdom, for he lies
  In Wisdom's arms. His wanderings are done,
  For he has found the Source whence all things run —
The guerdon of the quest, that satisfies.

He who knows Love becomes Love, and he knows
  All beings are himself, twin-born of Love.
Melted in Love's own fire, his spirit flows
  Into all earthly forms, below, above;
He is the breath and glamour of the rose,
  He is the benediction of the dove.

VISION
May Theilgaard Watts

To-day there have been lovely things
I never saw before;
Sunlight through a jar of marmalade;
A blue gate;
A rainbow
In soapsuds on dishwater;
Candlelight on butter;
The crinkled smile of a little girl
Who had new shoes with tassels;
A chickadee on a thorn-apple;
Empurpled mud under a willow,
Where white geese slept;
White ruffled curtains sifting moonlight
On the scrubbed kitchen floor;
The under side of a white-oak leaf;
Ruts in the road at sunset;
An egg yolk in a blue bowl.

My love kissed my eyes last night.

YOUR LITTLE VOICE
e.e. cummings

your little voice
                    Over the wires came leaping
and i felt suddenly
dizzy
          With the jostling and shouting of merry flowers
wee skipping high-heeled flames
courtesied before my eyes
                           or twinkling over to my side
Looked up
with impertinently exquisite faces
floating hands were laid upon me
I was whirled and tossed into delicious dancing
up
Up
with the pale important
                       stars and the Humorous
                            moon
dear girl
How i was crazy how i cried when i heard
                            over time
and tide and death
leaping
Sweetly
          your voice

PUT DOWN THE MAGAZINE
Rosemerry Wahtola Trommer

This night, come root for what we cannot know,
come hearken for the evening's pulse from where,
from where, let's do not care as long as there
is pulse, is pulse, and we can hear it grow
inside our pink desire, desire, the bow
of shoulds untied, shut blinds gape wide, the dare
to thirst defies both wrong and right. And bare
blank need, undress the sin, become sweet dough
of want and want and want and enter in
to evening, be its ears, become the sound
of something humming like the motor of
bright spheres revolving, deep hypnotic din
of yes, be curious, come join this round
our universe is chanting, love (oh!) love.

M *(from Relearning the Alphabet)*
Denise Levertov

Honest man, I wanted
      the moon and went
      out to sea to touch
      the moon and

      down a lane of bright
      broken vanishing
      curled pyramids of
      moonwater
      moving
      towards the moon
   and touched
   the luminous dissolving
   half moon
   cold

I am
come back,
humbled, to warm myself,
honest man,

our bed is
      upon the earth
your soul is
      in your body
your mouth
      has found
my mouth once more
      — I'm home.

I DREAMT THE GREEN HANDS OF THE CLOCK
Eileen D. Moeller

rolling backwards, merciful in their pull
toward the deep green days of our marriage,
of being luminous as a new shoot in your arms,
the puddle green of your kisses, the green tree-belly
moonlight over our bed, as the damp green song of peepers
frizzled the air, you on your knees above me, the Spanish
moss of your hair swaying as we rose in the soft growing
dance of love, those greenest moments of our conviction.

How sweet then, to awaken
fresh from a night like this, still beside you,
to stand rubbing our eyes in disbelief
as we look out the window at this fog,
thick and pale hydrangea green,
turning the buildings, everything, alien,
this lightning raging across the city on long white legs,
how sweet to feel as if we were just born yesterday,
the green hands of the clock rolling
backwards, merciful in their pull.

FIREFLIES
Rolf Jacobsen translated by Roger Greenwald

It was that evening with the fireflies
while we were waiting for the bus to Velletri
that we saw two old people kissing
under the plane tree. It was then
you said, half to the air
half to me:
Whoever loves for years
hasn't lived in vain.
And it was then I caught sight of the first
fireflies in the darkness, sparkling
with flashes of light around your head.
It was then.

MY FATHER'S HATS
Mark Irwin

Sunday mornings I would reach
high into his dark closet while standing
   on a chair and tiptoeing reach
higher, touching, sometimes fumbling
   the soft crowns and imagine
I was in a forest, wind hymning
   through pines, where the musky scent
of rain clinging to damp earth was
   his scent I loved, lingering on
bands, leather, and on the inner silk
   crowns where I would smell his
hair and almost think I was being
   held, or climbing a tree, touching
the yellow fruit, leaves whose scent
   was that of a clove in the godsome
air, as now, thinking of his fabulous
   sleep, I stand on this canyon floor
and watch light slowly close
   on water I'm not sure is there.

FACING IT
Shara McCallum

Always the same questions
of blood and bread breaking,
eaten in communion
with what we know — this chair,
the candle flickering.
With what we don't — the dark
outside the window, night
ashen like the voice of my hands.

If I could again be a child
at my mother's side,
I would believe in the stove,
the lit room; in her skirt
swishing against my face
as I crumpled the hem in my fist,
made my hand a flag to wave
my mother's love into my skin.

I once was lost
but now I'm found, she hummed.
And we were, she and I.
And I believed in the night
more fiercely, believed
in my mother, my hand wrapt
in her skirt, moving back and forth
across my face, her face, the face
of God, the face I loved.

TALKING TO MY SON BEFORE SLEEP
Rosemerry Wahtola Trommer

"Which is bigger," he asks me, "the ocean or sky,"
      and I want to tell him the heart, which even today
            has been practicing vastness, is learning to say yes

in new languages, learning to stretch beyond
      the center, beyond the lips, learning to be more moon
            and less woman, to reflect light without owning it,

learning to lose whatever it has used before as a measure.
      This is the way I want to love: in an idiom stronger
            than tongues. I want to love in the way that tides pull

and release, like the moon which holds without touch.
      I want to invite the sky to create a bigger space in me
            a place spacious enough to hold all the wings

of the passing moment. I want to be buoyant enough
      to carry all of love's weight. "The sky," I say.
            "The sky is bigger, but the ocean is also wide."

He is satisfied by my words, closes his eyes.
      In my chest, a star falls. In my belly
            strong tug of the tides.

MOTHER OF US ALL
Stephen Levine

Mother-of-us-all prays to free us
from our image of perfection
to which so much suffering clings.

When in the shadowy mind
we imagine ourselves imperfectly,
praying to be freed from gravity
by enlightenment, she refines our prayers.

Putting her arms around us
she bids us rest our head on her shoulder
whispering, Don't you know
with all your fear and anger
all you are fit for is love.

A BLESSING
James Wright

Just off the highway to Rochester, Minnesota,
Twilight bounds softly forth on the grass.
And the eyes of those two Indian ponies
Darken with kindness.
They have come gladly out of the willows
To welcome my friend and me.
We step over the barbed wire into the pasture
Where they have been grazing all day, alone.
They ripple tensely, they can hardly contain their happiness
That we have come.
They bow shyly as wet swans. They love each other.
There is no loneliness like theirs.
At home once more,
They begin munching the young tufts of spring in the darkness.
I would like to hold the slenderer one in my arms,
For she has walked over to me
And nuzzled my left hand.
She is black and white,
Her mane falls wild on her forehead,
And the light breeze moves me to caress her long ear
That is delicate as the skin over a girl's wrist.
Suddenly I realize
That if I stepped out of my body I would break
Into blossom.

IF YOU'RE WILLING
Rolf Jacobsen translated by Olav Grinde

Do you have enough
warmth?
You do.
Sleep, thoughts
are given you freely.
But the warmth inside you
you must give
and give again.

You too
can speak a word of joy.
You have a hand,
warm
if you're willing.

HOPE
Nicholas Mazza

Hope
is the belief
that one hand
reaching to another
can eventually
touch the moon,
allowing the light
to guide us
through the night.

MAY MY HEART ALWAYS BE OPEN TO LITTLE
e.e. cummings

may my heart always be open to little
birds who are the secrets of living
whatever they sing is better than to know
and if men should not hear them men are old

may my mind stroll about hungry
and fearless and thirsty and supple
and even if it's sunday may i be wrong
for whenever men are right they are not young

and may myself do nothing usefully
and love yourself so more than truly
there's never been quite such a fool who could fail
pulling all the sky over him with one smile

VI. How a Beautiful Day Is Spent

"Let the beauty that you love
be what you do."

JALĀL AD-DĪN RŪMĪ

SITTING UP WITH MY WIFE ON NEW YEAR'S EVE
Hsu Chun-Ch'ien *translated by Burton Watson*

So many delights the excitement has no end,
so much joy the cup is never still:
pluck a daddy longlegs out of the wine,
find a wild plum inside the dumpling!
The blinds swing open and wind lifts the curtain;
the candle burns low, its wick turned to ash.
No wonder the pins weigh heavily in your hair —
we've waited up so long for dawn light to come!
> *(It was a custom at New Year's to place a daddy longlegs,*
> *whose name, hzi-tzu, is a homophone for "happiness," in the wine,*
> *and to hide wild plums in the dumplings.)*

TRAVELING GATHA
Ziyong *translated by Beata Grant*

I still recall how, with my bag on a pole,
   I forgot my yesterdays,
Wandered the hills, played in the waters,
   went to the land of the clouds.
The lift of an eyebrow, the blink of an eye —
   all of it is samadhi;
In this great world there is nowhere that is
   not a wisdom hall.

SEARCHING FOR THE DHARMA
Hsu Yun *translated by the monks of the Zen Buddhist Order of Hsu Yun*

You've traveled up ten thousand steps in search of the Dharma.
So many long days in the archives, copying, copying.
The gravity of the Tang and the profundity of the Sung
make heavy baggage.
Here! I've picked you a bunch of wildflowers.
Their meaning is the same
but they're much easier to carry.

THAT WOULD REALLY BE SOMETHING
Rosemerry Wahtola Trommer

Sitting quietly, doing nothing, spring comes and the grass grows by itself.
—Zen proverb

I would like to make nothing
a verb. I nothing. You nothing.

We nothing. That second person
plural is my favorite conjugation.

Imagine. Both of us nothinging together.
Where? I don't care. The garden.

The alley. The canyon. The floor.
More nothing. Oh, it's nothing.

Nothing is sacred, anymore.
And there, on the altar of air

our minds and bodies rest. They unfold
in the hollow, the gaps. Though

when nothing happens, that's
all I want to talk about. I thrill

at nothing. I love nothing.
Nothing's perfect. Nothing's easy.

The grass continues to grow.
Nothing to do. Nothing to say.

Let's nothing together all day.

CATCH WHAT YOU CAN *(excerpt)*
Jean Garrigue

The thing to do is try for that sweet skin
One gets by staying deep inside a thing.
The image that I have is that of fruit—
The stone within the plum or some such pith
As keeps the slender sphere both firm and sound.

Stay with me, mountain flowers I saw
And battering moth against a wind-dark rock,
Stay with me till you build me all around
The honey and the clove I thought to taste
If lingering long enough I lived and got
Your intangible wild essence in my heart . . .

WEAVING A WORK
Pamela Cranston

White bowers
of spiced jasmine
drop their ringlets
of stars,
as night gently lifts
her black skirts,
as finches
spar with each other
over feeders stuffed
with thistle and corn.

Meanwhile, the steady thrum
of traffic rises,
relentless
as a stiff-necked wind,
that never heard about slack
or thought about pause,
which presses down
upon the world
until everything doubles back
upon itself.

Listen, I know how hard it is
to live carefree as lilies,
how hard for our hands to toil and spin
in this harried world, how the job
by four p.m. hangs heavy
as a bag of moans.

Pay attention to the ones
who find happiness in their work,
who know how to sift pure gold
from the slag-heap of days,
who work with a purpose,
and without haste —

like the diligent spider
who slips along her slender thread,
spooled from the cave
of her dexterous body. See
how she casts her gossamer
and dangerous net
into her ocean of sky, weaving
a work as if she had but one day
to live — and as if she had
a thousand years.

PASTORALE FOR SPRING
Al Zolynas

The new grass, the new lambs
eating the grass, the new calves
butting heads under the slow gaze
of bull-fathers beyond wire fences,
the sparrows flying with pieces of straw
in their beaks, the seagulls a thousand
miles from salt water eating worms
turned up by the plow,
the earth itself. . . .

                   It is not enough.
I go into the house and put on
Beethoven's 6th symphony, the Pastorale.
I listen to violins and oboes,
former trees, pretending to be winds,
birds and brooks. I listen to drums,
the hides of animals, trying to be
thunder.
It all works, somehow:

the thunder, controllable — a living room
thunder, and yet the living room a world, too.
Outside, the earth is being lifted
by the music, it is rising
out of itself, trees wave their arms
like mad conductors, the sky is breaking
into applause.

SAILING
Al Zolynas

After years by the ocean
a man finds he learns to sail
in the middle of the country,
on the surface of a small lake with a woman's name
in a small boat with one sail.

All summer he skims back and forth
across the open, blue eye of the midwest.
The wind comes in from the northeast
most days and the man learns
how to seem to go against it, learns
of the natural always crouched
in the shadow of the unnatural.

Sometimes the wind stops
and the man is becalmed —
just like the old traders who sat for days
in the doldrums on the thin skin of the ocean,
nursing their scurvys
and grumbling over short grog rations.

And the man learns a certain language:
he watches the luff, beats windward, comes
hard-about, finally gets
port and starboard straight.

All summer, between the soft, silt bottom
and the blue sheath of the sky, he glides
back and forth across the modest lake
with the woman's name.

And at night
he dreams of infinite flat surfaces,
of flying at incredible speed,
one hand on the tiller, one on the mainsheet, leaning
far out over the sparkling surface, the sail
a transparent membrane, the wind
with its silent howl, a force
moving him from his own heart.

THE ZEN OF HOUSEWORK
Al Zolynas

I look over my own shoulder
down my arms
to where they disappear under water
into hands inside pink rubber gloves
moiling among dinner dishes.

My hands lift a wine glass,
holding it by the stem and under the bowl.
It breaks the surface
like a chalice
rising from a medieval lake.

Full of the grey wine
of domesticity, the glass floats
to the level of my eyes.
Behind it, through the window
above the sink, the sun, among
a ceremony of sparrows and bare branches,
is setting in Western America.

I can see thousands of droplets
of steam — each a tiny spectrum — rising
from my goblet of grey wine.
They sway, changing directions
constantly — like a school of playful fish,
or like the sheer curtain
on the window to another world.

Ah, grey sacrament of the mundane!

DOMESTIC POEM
Eileen D. Moeller

nightfall I sink
into dishwash meditation
steaming china prayer wheels
crystalline bells of the lost horizon
crockery mandalas
chanting din and lull of running water
breathing slows
moist heat muscles soften
zen poems drip from silverware
my air humming out
in a cleansing melody
washing the frantic stew of a whole day
down the drain
along with the suds
those transient rainbow things
with the thin skin of
a passing instant

MAKING TORTILLAS *(excerpt)* for Liliana, "La Argentina"
Alicia Gaspar de Alba

My body remembers
what it means to love slowly,
what it means to start
from scratch:
to soak the maiz,
scatter bonedust in the limewater,
and let the seeds soften
overnight.

Sunrise is the best time
for grinding masa,
cornmeal rolling out
on the metate like a flannel sheet.
Smell of wet corn, lard, fresh
morning love and the light
sound of clapping.

                Pressed between the palms,
     clap-clap
                thin yellow moons—
     clap-clap
                still moist, heavy still
                from last night's soaking
     clap-clap
                slowly starting to find their shape
     clap-clap

My body remembers
the feel of the griddle,
beads of grease sizzling
under the skin, a cry gathering
like an air bubble in the belly
of the unleavened cake. Smell
of baked tortillas all over the house,
all over the hands still
hot from clapping, cooking...

HAIKU
Audrey Olberg

Summer gardening
Feel of the beet root
Beneath my ungloved hand

DAILY
Naomi Shihab Nye

These shriveled seeds we plant,
corn kernel, dried bean,
poke into loosened soil,
cover over with measured fingertips

These T-shirts we fold into
perfect white squares

These tortillas we slice and fry to crisp strips
This rich egg scrambled in a gray clay bowl

This bed whose covers I straighten
smoothing edges till blue quilt fits brown blanket
and nothing hangs out

This envelope I address
so the name balances like a cloud
in the center of the sky

This page I type and retype
This table I dust till the scarred wood shines
This bundle of clothes I wash and hang and wash again
like flags we share, a country so close
no one needs to name it

The days are nouns: touch them
The hands are churches that worship the world

WIND FILLS THEM
Eileen D. Moeller

Wind fills them
big as udders full of sweet milk.

She hangs the clothes
every day on the line like this,
arranging them all.
Her mother's flannel nightgowns
and black waitress uniforms,
then her father's heavy work shirts,
his dark green pants a forest of legs,
her brothers' dungarees
in three graduated sizes,
all with holes in the knees,
all their white socks
that won't wash clean.

She hangs them by the toes,
the hems, the legs,
joins them together
with the work of her fingers
and tight wooden pins.

She makes the music,
the pulley squeaking time
as she reels them out
as far as they can go.

And she is lifted
by the way they drink
the air in lusty gulps,
the way they catch and pull
each other this way, that way
in a lurching dance.

Here the family's
secret life takes flight
and she's opened the cage.

How nourished she feels,
how tender, and full of romance.

DEAR EZRA
Eileen D. Moeller

I have to confess:
there are abstractions
I no longer go in fear of.

Take loneliness.
I've started calling it solitude.
It feels so new and improved now,
I can honestly say it soaks up time
better than a sponge soaks up water.

The other day I actually washed this poem with it.

Ez, let me tell you,
aging is a Laundromat,
and eventually you find yourself
watching what you spurned
and dreaded for years
spread out in widening gyres,
like sheets fluffed in the dryer.

Life is quite a bit cozier
when you let all the bugaboos —
you know — say, sadness and fear
crawl into bed with you.

Pace them with your breathing
and they fall asleep
fast as a couple of kids.

The other night we huddled together
staring at the moon
as it slid past my window:
big-bellied sail on a wet black sea.

WHAT'S LEFT for Peter Hennessy
Kerry Hardie

I used to wait for the flowers,
my pleasure reposed on them.
Now I like plants before they get to the blossom.
Leafy ones — foxgloves, comfrey, delphiniums —
fleshy tiers of strong leaves pushing up
into air grown daily lighter and more sheened
with bright dust like the eyeshadow
that tall young woman in the bookshop wears,
its shimmer and crumble on her white lids.

The washing sways on the line, the sparrows pull
at the heaps of drying weeds that I've left around.
Perhaps this is middle age. Untidy, unfinished,
knowing there'll never be time now to finish,
liking the plants — their strong lives —
not caring about flowers, sitting in weeds
to write things down, look at things,
watching the sway of shirts on the line,
the cloth filtering light.

I know more or less
how to live through my life now.
But I want to know how to live what's left
with my eyes open and my hands open;
I want to stand at the door in the rain
listening, sniffing, gaping.
Fearful and joyous,
like an idiot before God.

WALKING A FIELD INTO EVENING
Larry Smith

For learned books, I read the grasses.
For reputation, a bird calls my name.
I cross a stone bridge with the pace of dusk.
At the meadow gate, six cows meditate.

For decades I ran with my mind up hill and down;
now idleness lets me see what is near.
An arrow of wild geese crosses the sky,
my body still, my feet firm on the ground.

We age like trees now, watch our seedlings
take wind or grow around us.
I'm going to mark my books lightly
with a pencil. When someone wants
to take my picture, I'll walk towards them
and embrace. No more arguments
just heart sense, or talk about nothing.
Take walks in the woods at dawn and dusk,
breathe in the damp musty air,
learn to listen before I die.

FROM BLOSSOMS
Li-Young Lee

From blossoms comes
this brown paper bag of peaches
we bought from the boy
at the bend in the road where we turned toward
signs painted *Peaches*.

From laden boughs, from hands,
from sweet fellowship in the bins,
comes nectar at the roadside, succulent
peaches we devour, dusty skin and all,
comes the familiar dust of summer, dust we eat.

O, to take what we love inside,
to carry within us an orchard, to eat
not only the skin, but the shade,
not only the sugar, but the days, to hold
the fruit in our hands, adore it, then bite into
the round jubilance of peach.

There are days we live
as if death were nowhere
in the background; from joy
to joy to joy, from wing to wing,
from blossom to blossom to
impossible blossom, to sweet impossible blossom.

THANKSGIVING
Rosemerry Wahtola Trommer

More than these greens tossed with toasted pecans,
I want to serve you the hymn I sung into the wooden bowl
as I blended the oil and white vinegar. More than honey ice cream
beside the warm pie, I want to serve you the bliss in the apples' flesh,
how it gathered the sun and carried its luminousness to this table.
More than the popovers, the risen ecstasy of wheat, milk and eggs,
I want to serve you the warmth that urged the transformation to bread.
Blessings, I want to serve you full choruses of hallelujah, oh so wholly
here in this moment. Oh so holy here in this world.

GRACE
Alice Walker

Grace
gives me a day
Too beautiful
I had thought
To stay indoors
& yet
Washing my dishes
Straightening
My shelves
Finally
Throwing out
The wilted
Onions
Shrunken garlic
Cloves
I discover
I am happy
To be inside
Looking out.
This, I think,
Is wealth.
Just this choosing
Of how
A beautiful day
Is spent.

VII. The All–Surrounding Grace

"The most beautiful experience we can have
is the mystical."

ALBERT EINSTEIN

ENLIGHTENMENT
Dogen Zenji *translated by Kazuaki Tanahashi*

Enlightenment is like the moon reflected on the water.
The moon does not get wet, nor is the water broken.
Although its light is wide and great,
The moon is reflected even in a puddle an inch wide.
The whole moon and the entire sky
Are reflected in dewdrops on the grass,
Or even in one drop of water.

TO LEARN THE SCRIPTURES
Lal Ded *translated by Jane Hirshfield*

To learn the scriptures is easy,
to live them, hard.
The search for the Real
is no simple matter.

Deep in my looking,
the last words vanished.
Joyous and silent,
the waking that met me there.

THE GREAT SEA
Uvavnuk *translated by Jane Hirshfield*

The great sea
frees me, moves me,
as a strong river carries a weed.
Earth and her strong winds
move me, take me away,
and my soul is swept up in joy.

ON THE BEACH AT NIGHT, ALONE
Walt Whitman

On the beach at night alone,
As the old mother sways her to and fro, singing her husky song,
As I watch the bright stars shining — I think a thought of the clef of
    the universes and of the future.

A vast similitude interlocks all,
All spheres, grown, ungrown, small, large, suns, moons, planets,
    comets, asteroids,
All the substances of the same, and all that is spiritual upon the same,
All distances of place, however wide,
All distances of time — all inanimate forms,
All Souls, all living bodies, though they be ever so different, or in
    different worlds,
All gaseous, watery, vegetable, mineral processes — the fishes, the brutes,
All nations, colors, barbarisms, civilizations, languages,
All identities that have existed, or may exist, on this globe, or any globe;
All lives and deaths — all of the past, present, future;
This vast similitude spans them, and always has spann'd,
    And shall forever span
them, and compactly hold them, and enclose them.

SAGESSE *(excerpt)*
H.D. – Hilda Doolittle

Or is it a great tide that covers the rock-pool
so that it and the rock are indistinguishable

from the sea-shelf and are part of the sea-floor,
though the sea anemone may quiver apprehensively

and the dried weed uncurl painfully
and the salt-sediment rebel, "I was salt,

a substance, concentrated, self-contained,
am I to be dissolved and lost?"

"it is fearful, I was a mirror, an individual,"
cries the shallow rock-pool, "now infinity

claims me; I am everything? But nothing";
peace, salt, you were never as useful as all that,

peace, flower, you are one of a thousand-thousand others,
peace, shallow pool, be lost.

NOW, IN THIS WANING OF LIGHT *(part 4 from "Meditation at Oyster River")*
Theodore Roethke

Now, in this waning of light,
I rock with the motion of morning;
In the cradle of all that is,
I'm lulled into half-sleep
By the lapping of water,
Cries of the sandpiper.
Water's my will, and my way,
And the spirit runs, intermittently,
In and out of the small waves,
Runs with the intrepid shorebirds —
How graceful the small before danger!

In the first of the moon,
All's a scattering,
A shining.

LATE FEAST
Adam Zagajewski

Evening, the edge of the city, a whole day
of void, then all at once
the late feast: the Sanskrit of dusk that speaks
in a glowing tongue of joy.
High overhead flow cigarette firelets
no one is smoking.
Sheets of blazing secrets aflame;
what the serenely fading sky tells
can't be remembered or even described.
So what if Pharaoh's armies pursue you,
when eternity is woven
through the days of the week like moss
in the chinks of a cabin?

THREE TIMES MY LIFE HAS OPENED
Jane Hirshfield

Three times my life has opened.
Once, into darkness and rain.
Once, into what the body carries at all times within it and starts
    to remember each time it enters the act of love.
Once, to the fire that holds all.
These three were not different.
You will recognize what I am saying or you will not.
But outside my window all day a maple has stepped from her leaves
    like a woman in love with winter, dropping the colored silks.
Neither are we different in what we know.
There is a door. It opens. Then it is closed. But a slip of light
    stays, like scrap of unreadable paper left on the floor,
    or the one red leaf the snow releases in March.

GLIMPSE
Chase Twichell

It was as if a window suddenly blew open
and the sky outside the mind came flooding in.
My childhood shriveled to a close,

thread of smoke that rose
and touched a cloud — or the cloud's

replica adrift on the slow river of thinking —
and disappeared inside it. In that dark water,
a new lily was opening, sky-white out of the muck.

It was only a glimpse, quick,
like a bird ruffling,

but I saw the flower's
beautiful stark shape, an artichoke
brightened from within by the moon.

A path lay shadowy at my feet,
and I followed it.

ONE EVENING
William Stafford

On a frozen pond a mile north of Liberal
almost sixty years ago I skated wild circles
while a strange pale sun went down.

A scattering of dry brown reeds cluttered
the ice at one end of the pond, and a fitful
breeze ghosted little surface eddies of snow.

No house was in sight, no tree, only
the arched wide surface of the earth
holding the pond and me under the sky.

I would go home, confront all my years, the tangled
events to come, and never know more than I did
that evening waving my arms in the lemon-colored light.

NEAR THE WALL OF A HOUSE
Yehuda Amichai translated by *Chana Block & Stephen Mitchell*

Near the wall of a house painted
to look like stone,
I saw visions of God.

A sleepless night that gives others a headache

gave me flowers
opening beautifully inside my brain.

And he who was lost like a dog
will be found like a human being
and brought back home again.

Love is not the last room: there are others
after it, the whole length of the corridor
that has no end.

BUDDHA, BIRDBATH, HANGING PLANT
Peter Skrzynecki

Three things stopped him in his stride
when he stepped out
into the garden — three things
under the great peppercorn
that he planted years ago:
the statue of a Buddha,
a birdbath and a plant in a basket
hanging from one of the peppercorn's branches.

The Buddha pointed to the earth,
to the "here and now."
The birdbath, filled with water,
reflected the tree above it.
The plant, a flowering hoya,
hung over the Buddha and birdbath like a crown.

His time of sorrow
vanished — as if pain and fear
had been nothing more than vapours
trailing through his imagination.
Somewhere from out of an ancient past,
he heard a voice, "The centre of the universe
is a bellylaugh."
The Buddha smiled; the water
in the birdbath rippled;
the hoya stirred
in a circular motion.

He stepped back, startled —
as if someone had pushed him.
Then he saw the great tree itself.

BUDDHA IN GLORY
Rainer Maria Rilke *translated by Stephen Mitchell*

Center of all centers, core of cores,
almond self-enclosed, and growing sweet —
all this universe, to the furthest stars
all beyond them, is your flesh, your fruit.

Now you feel how nothing clings to you;
your vast shell reaches into endless space,
and there the rich, thick fluids rise and flow.
Illuminated in your infinite peace,

a billion stars go spinning through the night,
blazing high above your head.
But in you is the presence that
will be, when all the stars are dead.

POETRY *(excerpt)*
Pablo Neruda *translated by Alistair Reid*

...I did not know what to say, my mouth
had no way
with names,
my eyes were blind,
and something started in my soul,
fever or forgotten wings,
and I made my own way,
deciphering
that fire,
and I wrote the first faint line,
faint, without substance, pure
nonsense,
pure wisdom
of someone who knows nothing,
and suddenly I saw
the heavens
unfastened
and open,
planets,
palpitating plantations,
shadow perforated,
riddled
with arrows, fire and flowers,
the winding night, the universe.

And I, infinitesimal being,
drunk with the great starry
void,
likeness, image of
mystery,
I felt myself a pure part
of the abyss,
I wheeled with the stars,
my heart broke loose on the wind.

IN THE BOOK
William Stafford

A hand appears.
It writes on the wall.
Just a hand moving in the air,
and writing on the wall.

A voice comes and says the words,
"You have been weighed,
you have been judged,
and have failed."

The hand disappears, the voice
fades away into silence.
And a spirit stirs and fills
the room, all space, all things.

All this in The Book
asks, "What have you done wrong?"
But The Spirit says,
"Come to me, who need comfort."

And the hand, the wall, the voice
are gone, but The Spirit is everywhere.
The story ends inside the book,
But outside, wherever you are —

It goes on.

AT THE CANCER CLINIC
Ted Kooser

She is being helped toward the open door
that leads to the examining rooms
by two young women I take to be her sisters.
Each bends to the weight of an arm
and steps with the straight, tough bearing
of courage. At what must seem to be
a great distance, a nurse holds the door,
smiling and calling encouragement.
How patient she is in the crisp white sails
of her clothes. The sick woman
peers from under her funny knit cap
to watch each foot swing scuffing forward
and take its turn under her weight.
There is no restlessness or impatience
or anger anywhere in sight. Grace
fills the clean mold of this moment
and all the shuffling magazines grow still.

FIRST LESSON
Philip Booth

Lie back, daughter, let your head
be tipped back in the cup of my hand.
Gently, and I will hold you. Spread
your arms wide, lie out on the stream
and look high at the gulls. A dead-
man's-float is face down. You will dive
and swim soon enough where this tidewater
ebbs to the sea. Daughter, believe
me, when you tire on the long thrash
to your island, lie up, and survive.
As you float now, where I held you
and let go, remember when fear
cramps your heart what I told you:
lie gently and wide to the light-year
stars, lie back, and the sea will hold you.

THE AVOWAL
Denise Levertov

As swimmers dare
to lie face to the sky
and water bears them,
as hawks rest upon air
and air sustains them,
so would I learn to attain
freefall, and float
into Creator Spirit's deep embrace,
knowing no effort earns
that all-surrounding grace.

THE PEACE OF WILD THINGS
Wendell Berry

When despair for the world grows in me
and I wake in the night at the least sound
in fear of what my life and my children's lives may be,
I go and lie down where the wood drake
rests in his beauty on the water, and the great heron feeds.
I come into the peace of wild things
who do not tax their lives with forethought
of grief. I come into the presence of still water.
And I feel above me the day-blind stars
waiting for their light. For a time
I rest in the grace of the world, and am free.

EAGLE POEM
Joy Harjo

To pray you open your whole self
To sky, to earth, to sun, to moon
To one whole voice that is you.
And know there is more
That you can't see, can't hear;
Can't know except in moments
Steadily growing, and in languages
That aren't always sound but other
Circles of motion.
Like eagle that Sunday morning
Over Salt River. Circled in blue sky
In wind, swept our hearts clean
With sacred wings.
We see you, see ourselves and know
That we must take the utmost care
And kindness in all things.
Breathe in, knowing we are made of
All this, and breathe, knowing
We are truly blessed because we
Were born, and die soon, within a
True circle of motion,
Like eagle rounding out the morning
Inside us.
We pray that it will be done
In beauty.
In beauty.

RECOMMENDED ANTHOLOGIES

MULTIPLE-POET Anthologies
of Spiritual Poetry

A Book of Luminous Things: An International Anthology of Poetry, edited by
Czeslaw Milosz , copyright © 1998 by Mariner Books.

Claiming the Spirit Within: A Sourcebook of Women's Poetry, edited by Marilyn Sewell,
copyright © 1996 by Beacon Press.

Cries of the Spirit: A Celebration of Women's Spirituality, edited by Marilyn Sewell,
copyright © 1991 by Beacon Press.

Evensong: Contemporary American Poets on Spirituality, edited by Gerry LaFemina
and Chad Prevost, copyright © 2006 by Bottom Dog Press.

Women in Praise of the Sacred: 43 Centuries of Poetry by Women, edited by
Jane Hirshfield, copyright © 1994 by Harper-Collins.

SINGLE-POET Anthologies
Concerning Yoga and Meditation

Faulds, Danna, (published by Peaceable Kingdom Books)
    From Root to Bloom: Yoga Poems and Other Writings, copyright © 2006.
    Go In and In: Poems From the Heart of Yoga, copyright © 2002.
    Limitless: New Poems and Other Writings, copyright © 2009.
    One Soul: More Poems From the Heart of Yoga, copyright © 2003.
    Prayers to the Infinite: New Yoga Poems, copyright © 2004.

Lowitz, Leza, *Yoga Poems: Lines to Unfold By,* copyright © 2006 by
Stone Bridge Press.

Ruvinsky, Joan, *This Wind,* copyright © 1998 by The Muses' Company.

Shaw, Fran, PhD, *Writing My Yoga: Poems for Presence,* copyright © 2009 by
Indications Press.

Twichell, Chase, *The Snow Watcher,* copyright © 1998 by Ontario Review Books.

PERMISSIONS

"Girls Take Their Stances" by **Janet Aalfs**. Reprinted with the permission of the author.

"Noisy Falling In." by **Janet Aalfs**, from *Reach*, copyright © 1999 by Perugia Press, www.perugiapress.com, and Janet Aalfs. Reprinted with the permission of the author.

"Making Tortillas" (excerpt) by **Alicia Gaspar de Alba**, from *Three Times a Woman: Chicana Poetry* by Alicia Gaspar de Alba, Maria Herrera-Sobek, and Demetria Martinez, copyright © 1989 by Bilingual Review Press. Reprinted with the permission of Bilingual Review Press www.asu.edu/brp.

"Near the Wall of a House" by **Yehuda Amichai**, from *The Selected Poetry of Yehuda Amichai*, translated and edited by Chana Bloch and Stephen Mitchell, copyright © 1996 by University of California Press. Reprinted with the permission of University of California Press, http://www.ucpress.edu.

"Fire" by **Muhyiddin ibn 'Arabi** , from *The Tarjuman Al Ashwaq* by Muhyi al-Din Muhammad ibn 'Ali Ibn al-'Arabi, translated by Reynold A. Nicholson, copyright © 1978 by Theosophical Books Ltd. Reprinted with the permission of Theosophical Books Ltd.

"You There" by **Judith Barrington**, from *Horses and the Human Soul* by Judith Barrington (Ashland, OR: Story Line Press, 2004), copyright © 2004 by Judith Barrington. Reprinted with the permission of the author, www.judithbarrington.com.

"Not without Longing" by **Karen Benke**, from *Sister* by Karen Benke, copyright © 2004 by Confl:X Press. Reprinted with the permission of the author, www.karenbenke.com.

"Sabbath Poem (2001 – IV)" by **Wendell Berry**, from *Given: Poems by Wendell Berry*, copyright © 2006 by Counterpoint Press. Reprinted with the permission of Counterpoint Press, www.counterpointpress.com.

"Sabbath Poem (1990 –V)"by **Wendell Berry**, from *A Timbered Choir*, copyright © 1999 by Counterpoint Press. Reprinted with the permission of Counterpoint Press, www.counterpointpress.com.

"The Peace of Wild Things" by **Wendell Berry**, from *The Selected Poems of Wendell Berry*, copyright © 1999 by Counterpoint Press. Reprinted with the permission of Counterpoint Press, www.counterpointpress.com.

"First Lesson" by **Phillip Booth**, from *Letter to a Distant Land* by Phillip Booth, copyright © 1957 by Phillip Booth. Reprinted with the permission of Viking Penguin, a division of Penguin Group (USA) Inc., http://us.penguingroup.com/static/pages/publishers/adult/viking.html.

"turning" by **Lucille Clifton**, from *Good Woman: Poems and a Memoir 1969-1980*, copyright © 1987 by Lucille Clifton. Reprinted with the permission of BOA Editions, Ltd., www.boaeditions.org.

"Prayer" (excerpts) by **Lisa Colt**, from *Claiming the Spirit Within: A Sourcebook of Women's Poetry*, edited by Marilyn Sewell, copyright © 1996 by Beacon Press, www.beacon.org. Reprinted with the permission of the author.

"On Putnam Brook Bridge" and "Weaving a Work" by **Pamela Cranston**, from *Coming to Treeline: Adirondack Poems by Pamela Cranston*, copyright © 2005 by St. Hubert's Press, www.sthubertspress.com. Reprinted with the permission of the author.

"This Body" by **Michael Cuddihy**, copyright © 1996 by Michael Cuddihy. Reprinted with the permission of Mary Cuddihy.

"your little voice/over the wires came leaping" by **e.e. cummings**, copyright ©1923, 1951, © 1991 by the Trustees for the E.E. Cummings Trust, copyright © 1976 by George James Firmage, "may my heart always be open to little" by e.e. cummings. Copyright © 1938, © 1966, 1991 by the Trustees for the E.E. Cummings Trust, from *Complete Poems 1904-1964 by e.e. cummings*, edited by George J. Firmage. Reprinted with the permission of Liveright Publishing Corporation.

"Enlightenment" by **Dogen Zenji**, from *Moon on a Dewdrop: Writings of Zen Master Dogen*, edited by Kaziaki Tanahashi, copyright © 1985 by the San Francisco Zen Center. Reprinted with the permission of North Point Press, a division of Farrar, Straus and Giroux, LLC.

"After" by **G.F. Dutton**, from *The Bare Abundance: Selected Poems 1975-2001* by G.F Dutton, Bloodaxe Books, copyright © 2002 by G.F. Dutton. Reprinted with the permission of Bloodaxe Books, www.bloodaxebooks.com.

"Just for Now" (excerpt) by **Danna Faulds**, from *Prayers to the Infinite*, copyright © 2004 by Peaceable Kingdom Books. Reprinted with the permission of the author.

INDEX OF POETS

INDEX OF POEMS AND FIRST LINES

CPSIA information can be obtained at www.ICGtesting.com
232690LV00002B/23/P

9 781432 734343